The Big Book of Woodworking Crafts for Beginners

DIY Woodwork Ideas With Step by Step Woodworking Projects and Plans Including Tips, Tools and Essential Techniques to Get You Started

By

Luke Byrd

Copyright © 2021 – Luke Byrd

All rights reserved

No part of this publication may be reproduced, distributed, or transmitted in any form or by any means, including photocopying, recording, or other electronic or mechanical methods, without the prior written permission of the publisher, except in the case of brief quotations embodied in reviews and certain other non-commercial uses permitted by copyright law.

Disclaimer

This publication is designed to provide competent and reliable information regarding the subject matter covered. However, the views expressed in this publication are those of the author alone, and should not be taken as expert instruction or professional advice. The reader is responsible for his or her own actions.

The author hereby disclaims any responsibility or liability whatsoever that is incurred from the use or application of the contents of this publication by the purchaser or reader. The purchaser or reader is hereby responsible for his or her own actions.

Table of Contents

Introduction 6

Chapter 1 10

Essentials of Woodworking 10

    What is Woodworking? 11

    History of Woodworking? 15

    Types of Woodworking 18

    Benefit of Woodworking 19

Chapter 2 23

Woodworking Processes and Techniques 23

Chapter 3 37

Woodworking Tips and Tricks 37

Chapter 4 54

Getting Started with Woodworking 54

    Basic Woodworking Tools and Supplies 54

        Wood 55

        Workbench 61

- Saw 63
- Hand Plane 70
- Orbital Sander 73
- Hand Files 74
- Vises 74
- Hammer 75
- Mallets 75
- Power Drill 76
- Screw Gun 76
- Squares 77
- Tape measures 78
- Wood Putty 79
- Setting Up Your Woodworking Workshop 80
- Woodworking Safety Tips and Maintenance 84

Chapter 5 89

Woodworking Projects Ideas 89

- Kitchen Board 89
- Picture Frame 93
- Wooden Arrow 96
- Doormat 99
- Bird Nest 101
- Pet Bed 105

Bow 110

Quick Box with Box Joints 115

Returnable Boomerang 120

Bandsaw Box 122

Floating Wine Bottle Holder 127

Chapter 6 132

Fixing Common Woodworking Problems 132

Chapter 7 143

Woodworking Frequently Asked Questions 143

Conclusion 151

Introduction

Crafts can be very fascinating, especially when it is something you can do without so many hassles and in your convenient time. It gets more interesting when you are crafting what you can personally use and directly beneficial to you. It is also strongly motivating when it is a craft you can make money from.

Woodworking is an all-round fascinating and interesting craft that allows you to make your own wooden household furniture and decorative pieces. It is also a craft you can monetize and make a career of.

Woodworking is beyond sawing, drilling and hitting nails on wood, as many people suppose. You need to familiarize yourself with a number of technicalities before you can successfully make a woodwork project. Although these technicalities are not difficult to master, you need to pay keen attention to them to avoid making grievous mistakes in your project.

Well, this is why you are reading this book – to learn, I believe.

I am glad you actually took the initiative to learn before you commence woodworking. Some folks just run off with their passion for creativity and end up with many catastrophes.

Truthfully, mistakes are almost inevitable in woodworking, but there are tricks to avoid them and also correct them when they occur. This will save you from accumulating scraps from mistaken projects. By following the instructions highlighted in this book, you are 98% covered from making costly mistakes in woodworking.

You also get to avoid a number of accidents and injuries a lot of persons encounter in the workshop. The workshop can be quite a dangerous place because of the type of risky tools stored there. In as much as you don't need a grand building for a workshop, you can't woodwork everywhere and anywhere. You need to get a space that will allow you to store all of your tools in order, move around easily, and work freely without endangering yourself.

Your workshop should also be very comfortable and weather friendly. You don't want to move your tools about during change of seasons. Though the workshop doesn't have to be a permanent place, it should be able to accommodate you for a long time, as consistent movement of tools and wood can reduce its quality.

Safety should be your number one check when woodworking; there is no value for creativity when you encounter a hazard.

All the same, you need to hone your creative abilities to make unique wooden projects and scale through mistakes.

To many people, woodworking is not just a craft to create a piece of furniture, but for some, it is a hobby through which they exercise their creativity.

If you are a highly productive person, this is a good place to put your productivity and creativity to work.

Woodworking is only easy when you are well equipped with the right measure and quality of knowledge.

However, before you rush into digesting the pages of this book, have in mind that this craft is highly rewarding if you are devoted to creativity, productivity, and hard work. Indeed, it is no lazy man's work.

First off, you have to eliminate every thought of perfection. Most struggling woodworking amateurs are being stunted by their excessive flare for perfection. Perfection comes with experience and professionalism, so give yourself wholeheartedly to learning the tidbits of this craft before chasing perfection.

Sincerely, there are so many things to woodworking that you need to discover before you commence the journey. This book has enlisted them in the most engaging and educating manner. You are bound to fall deeply in love with woodwork on the pages of this book. I wish you good luck.

Chapter 1

Essentials of Woodworking

Have you looked at a woodwork or furniture and conclude that it is only a jumble of nails, screws and wood? That is a very costly assumption of woodworking, as woodworking is more technical and very deep than nails and screws. However, we will be starting from the very basics to make things clear for you.

Woodworking represents different things to different folks. To some, it is a hobby, and to others, it is their lifelong profession. The hobbyist is just fascinated and in love with creating beautiful and very useful woodwork for themselves or others. The professional is also passionate to create woodwork for others but aims to get paid. Either gets highly rewarded for their skills and passion. The hobbyist mostly receives satisfaction from the appraisals his work brings. For them, it matters enough that someone complimented the slightest furniture they made. Also, using the furniture or piece they created gives them enough satisfaction. In the same vein, the professional derives reward for his passion and labors from the payment he gets. Anyone can be both! Yeah! You can be a professional woodworking hobbyist. It is very possible to make money from your passion/hobby.

However, whatever category you fall in, woodworking is a beautiful and highly productive craft that I'll encourage everyone to learn. Talk about being able to build your own furniture and meeting your own woodwork demands. Save more money with little stress. Also, it could be fun, well, that is if you know what you need to know.

With a well-balanced and foundational knowledge on woodworking, you can make money from making simple woodworks. Well, how is this possible? We have to lay the foundation for knowledge first. Woodworking can be quite tricky and technical. In this chapter, we will be looking at the aesthetic properties of woodworking.

What is Woodworking?
This is the art of making things from wood; it includes carpentry and furniture. It is the creation of objects

using wood and power tools. It is a woodwork craft that will forever remain fresh in your head. It can also be challenging as you evolve.

This is an exciting craft for those who believe they can do things with their hands. If you are into creativity, this is a field you can engage in to build your creativity.

Someone anonymously said, "woodworking minus patience equals firewood." Without patience, you won't be able to make any headway in the woodworking industry. Your projects will always go wrong and you'll always get frustrated.

Woodworking is mostly about creativity, perception and patience. Without these three, you cannot make any tangible progress in the industry.

It can be quite diversifying; it includes anything from general carpentry to detailed woodworking.

Woodworking can be hard work. It is hard work when you are bankrupt of the right quality of knowledge.

This craft encompasses all form of furniture building and wooden project that involves the joining of wood with nails or joints or adhesives, and holding structures together with nails or screws.

Every project in woodworking is unique and involves its own unique process and techniques. Every project ought to begin with rigorous design and planning. To be a good woodworker, the craftsman must be a very good strategic thinker, a smart planner, calculative and detailed person.

Also, he should be skilled in mending and rebuilding damaged woodworks.

Things a woodworker makes includes:

- Boats
- Shelves, furniture
- Windows, doors
- Animal housing
- Workbenches
- Utensils
- Picture frames
- Toys

Under these products that a woodworker can make, we have so many categories of woodworking. These categories of woodworking were created of recent.

From the beginning, there has been no category of woodwork, every woodworker was expected to be a jack of all woodworks and so it was. However, the craft's only distinctions were the interior and exterior woodwork (carpentry and bench joining). They are usually referred to as more technical and challenging. Today, different forms of woodworking have been developed, thus exposing us to several specialties in woodworking; some of them are; chair makers, shipwrights, woodcarvers, barrel makers, wheelwrights, and instrument makers. These forms of woodworking are very deep and technical.

Each of these specialties has its different tools, tricks, and strategies used in the making process. Thus, we can say woodworking is very large and highly demanding craft. To make it a profession, you'll have to engage in more strategic woodworking. You can select one of these specialties and major in it, but you need to be educated on woodworking basics before you do that. They will be discussed extensively in other chapters.

However, it is said that if you want to understand the technicality of a thing, check its genesis. The history of woodworking is quite an interesting story being that it is an age-long act.

History of Woodworking?

Man discovered wood as early as he discovered agriculture. Wood is a product of trees. Man used these trees to build shelter for himself by cutting down the trees and breaking them into small pieces to make something reasonable for their survival. Before man started living in concrete and bricks houses, wood was the main resource man used in building. Some persons still live in wood houses, but it is not so popular today.

Well, man has always been a creative creature with sharp development insights. Thus, it wasn't difficult for him to master the art and specialize in it.

The discovery of making objects using tree wood seems magical. Who could have thought?! Different materials have been made from different combinations of various woodwork materials.

It was everybody's craft. Back then, anyone could make their own tools through the simple process of hitting and hammering.

Just like stone, clay and animal parts, wood was one of the things man first worked on. It was one early craft that many persons were involved in. it was quite common amongst local settlers.

The development of woodworking skills also led to civilization. As civilization grew, so did woodworking. There were several foreign tools and techniques that were introduced. This was what encouraged the growth of the woodworking industry and the advancement thereof. Different methods of woodworking have been developed over the years.

Tracing woodworking down to a particular time can be very difficult, as there was advancement in different places.

Woodworking became more advanced in Germany in 1568, bow saw and planning.

In Germany, local settlers began making wooden tools and weapons like spear

Neolithic times introduced carved wooden vessels.

Northern Germany and Denmark turned tree trunks in coffins, wooden folding-chair. Fellbach-Schmieden in

Germany has a lot of fine examples of wooden animal statues from the Iron Age.

Ancient Egypt also made many Egyptian drawings and many ancient Egyptian furniture (such as stools, chairs, tables, beds, chests) from wood. Some of these things are still being preserved today. Their coffins were also made of wood.

The progenitors of Chinese woodworking are Lu ban and his wife Lady Yun from 771 to 476BC. His teachings are supposedly left behind in the book Lu Ban Jing. (Manuscript of Lu Ban). Despite this, it is believed that the book was written 1500 years after his death.

Computer Numeric Controlled (CNC) machines have been developed to handle most woodworking tasks. It can carve complicated and detailed shapes into flat signs and art into different designs. Some of these machines are rechargeable power tools. In making designated projects like boring holes, it makes the project easier and faster. Although there are still demands for handcraft like in furniture making.

Over the years, people began to learn more advanced skills, techniques, and wood project strategies. Then, it became a well-recognized art. The making of artworks from tools is known as parquetry, marquetry, wood carving and cabinetry. That was the beginning of the advancement in the wood making world.

Types of Woodworking

You would notice that there are different types of woodwork around; this is because most of them pass through different processes. Some appear to be more challenging, engaging and appealing than others. The uniqueness of woodworking is that there are so many varieties to it. This variety is a result of the different wood available; each tree is a different wood. See below for example;

1. Woodcarving: use of a cutting tool to make a figure or sculpture from a wood.
2. Woodturning: a form of woodworking used to create objects on a lathe. The wood is moving while a stationary tool is used to cut and shape it.
3. Pyrography: Decorating wood with burn marks from a heated object. It is also called poke work.
4. Scroll sawing: this is the use of a scroll saw to cut intricate shapes in a thin wood. The scrollsaw has

thin blades that are used in cutting small and delicate cuts.
5. Wood mosaics: the design of wood with illusions or impressions. There are two types of wood mosaic
6. Construction: under this, we have furniture, boxes, repair and restoration (skills)
   a. Furniture: from the basic 3-legged stool to detailed cabinetry. Furniture has grown very wide, interesting and complex.
   b. Boxes: this is a functional and decorative piece. It sometimes includes different techniques to make like sawing, turning and joining.
   c. Repair and restoration: a preservation skill that involves knowledge of ordinary construction skills like joining.

Benefit of Woodworking

Even if you don't intend to make a career out of woodworking, you can build your woodwork to your taste and at your pace.

Woodworking saved a lot earlier. Man was able to access more comfort from his woodwork products, tools for battle, tools for farming to grow crops and build the earliest transport system via water. This is an important process that led to the advancement of civilization. Below are some other benefits of woodworking.

1. Satisfaction: the satisfaction and pride of building something with your hands can be thrilling
2. It helps you build muscle: the process of woodworking can give you the space to stretch some muscles and exercise.
3. It can improve your math skill: woodworking could be quite calculative and could demand some addition of arithmetic during measurements. To make a perfect woodwork, you need to make accurate arithmetic and calculations.
4. It improves your skillset: to make quality progress in life, you need to have a good skillset. Your skillset shouldn't just consist of many tools, but helpful tools that can improve the quality of your life. Having woodworking as a skill could be very resourceful and helpful to save cost of

purchasing new furniture or mending the damaged one. This doesn't only help you save money but the opportunity to build expertise in a lifelong skill. There are also a number of individual skills and tools that are involved in wood making. You will learn how to improve yourself

5. It enhances your creative development: woodworking is a creative art. To engage in it at any level, you need to be creative. In the learning process, you get to come across a lot of challenging projects that you can only handle creatively. You must not know everything at first. However, once you get into the craft, your creativity will be greatly enhanced. As soon as you get deeper into the craft, you'll start creating projects of your own. You could come up with projects of your own and fully design it yourself. You'll also need to sort out problems you may run into during a project, hence working your mind towards being creative. Woodworking will expose your mind to so many possibilities.

6. It increases mental sharpness: it is a mind exercising craft.

7. It reduces stress; many think that carpentry is a stress reliever.
8. You'll learn strong motor control.
9. It improves your literacy.
10. It boosts your mood; making wood projects can be fun

Chapter 2

Woodworking Processes and Techniques

Woodworking can be a tasking and rewarding job. It is more of a painstaking job when you are oblivious of the techniques need to make your project turn out exactly how you want it. The processes can be quite energy demanding and challenging. You have to follow an orderly plan to ensure that your project turns out as you expected. No one just walks into the workshop and clicks his fingers to magically make appear that which he /she desires.

To be successful in every craft, you have to be plan and organize; you need to be sure about the project you intend making. You need to create a plan, draw out how you expect the project to turn out and the basic steps to put in place.

Processes involved in woodworking:

- Create a plan

The very first step in woodworking is drawing a plan.

You should have decided what project you want to create by now. Now, go on to draft a plan.

How do you start? Where do you make curves and bends? Where do you do the joinery.

- Check your material list

Write a comprehensive list of what you need. Go after the list again, even when you must have highlighted everything. This will guide the project you will be making and guarantee that the project is a success.

- Premill all the boards to get straight and flat boards

Go through all your woods and choose the flat side that matches color combination, sizes and shapes. Select the right wood sizes so that you won't have to resume shaping and sawing before joining. Ensure the woods are well aligned. Mill the boards to their equal dimensions by planing and jointing. Cut the joints. Dry fit the assemblies and subassemblies before applying glue. Glue the assemblies and clamp them. Work very quickly.

Clamp carefully so that the two joints are well fitted.

Square the parts until you get a perfect shape of what you want. Check if the woods are diagonally aligned. Also, check for flatness.

After now, you can go ahead with your other projects. Each project has unique steps that makes the design turn out the way it does. You can go ahead to other steps in your projects.

NB: A project might require special procedures that you are not so familiar with. Feel free to adjust to the systems of the project.

In this book, we will be looking at a number of projects and not all of them will follow these steps. So don't allow yourself to be stereotyped. Creativity is usually born out of the box, don't get yourself stuck in the box. However, there are a number of techniques you are sure to come across during your woodworking exercise. It is almost impossible for you to complete a project without involving one of these techniques. These techniques are very common and basic.

Below is a list of the techniques. I'll explain them in clear details to you and have them at the side of your mind. These are not hard techniques at all; they are very basic and simple.

- Sawing: Sawing means dividing through a wood with a saw. It is the act of cutting wood into various shapes and sizes. As the saw blade comes in contact with the wood, it tears it at that point and creates an obvious division. There are many types of saws used in woodworking, each of them carrying out a particular task. The angle at which the saw meets the wood determines the grain pattern of the wood and how it will eventually turn out. Depending on the type of saw used, there are different sawing methods. A number of them are general saws that can be used for virtually every type of sawing. I'll be introducing you to these saws in chapter four. There are different ways of sawing; it brings about different shapes and looks of wood and for different purposes.

Quarter sawing: The wood is first cut plainly by passing the saw blade through the wood; the wood is cut into quarters and sawn into smaller quarters. A quarter board is sawn in one face; the other board is sawn in an opposite face. This sawing method aims to yield vertical and uniform grain patterns in a wood, leading to fewer boards per log.

Rift sawing: The wood is first cut into quarters just like in the above case and each quarter is sawn with growth rings at 30 to 60 degree angles. It has a similar look with the quarter sawn wood.

Plain sawing: This is flat sawing where the saw leaves no special indention on the wood and the line runs straight down without any holding back to it. This is the most common type of sawing, where the saw is passed through the wood once with no indention.

Saw dust is one common thing associated with sawing; you can't take it away, no matter the tool you use. Some saws might reduce the saw dust level, but it doesn't totally eliminate the saw dust.

- Sanding: This is a process that involves the smoothing of the surface of a wood using sandpapers. There are different shapes, sizes and forms of sandpapers. Each of these sandpapers serves peculiar purposes. Sandpapers are not the only smoothing tools used in woodworking, but they are one of the commonest and oldest. Before other smoothing tools came about, sanding was done majorly through sandpapers. Technology introduced files, planes and scrapers. Sanding works for all woods; while the rest of these tools work well with hardwoods, they could cut deep into softwoods and that'll become a problem you can't fix. They are also used to reduce the size of the wood. In place of a swing, you can use a plane to reduce the width of a drawer so it fits into the cabinet. It is a much easier and safer means of reducing the size of wood than using a saw. These tools are made with abrasive materials that can scrap or file the wood surface when it comes to contact. These abrasive materials are made to be very sharp, almost as sharp as a blade. However, there are different levels of sharpness of abrasives. I would advise that you use the sharpest abrasive at the beginning, then switch to softer ones at the end or towards the finishing. Sanding is not only done to smoothen the surface of a wood but also to reduce the effect or color of a point after the finishing. It is also done to reduce the dullness of a wood.

- Machining: This is the process after the wood has been dried. A wet wood should not be machined. This involves sawing the wood into a furniture final shape, e.g the leg. The process of sawing begins with rough planing to cut off saw and rip saw to final planing, to moulding, lathing and table sawing. These tools used in machining also lead to material removal. However, it is not wasteful like sawing. Machining in lay mans' words will be altering the shape, size and surface quality of a wood. This technique is used mainly in the production of chips for chipboard. Machining is usually done before the finishing stage. When machining, avoid using excess cutting pressure. Standard cutting pressure could split a natural wood along the grain and result in plucking and tearing.

- Bending: The design of a project could require bending certain wood parts. This technique is quite technical and appears to be very tricky. You don't have to be tricked into believing it is not something you can do. Bending a wood to make into furniture can be done through steam. This process is called steam bending. Steam bending is a technique where wood is exposed to the heat from steam. The moisture from the steam can soften the wood fibers so that it is possible to bend without being broken. You can bend the wood by stretching the wood into the shape you intend. However, you will have to be careful when bending the wood and exert a little pressure to prevent it from getting broken. Presently, you don't need to be struggling to trap steam. The wood is placed in a steam box until it is soft enough to be bent. The very first product of steam bending is the rocking chair in the 18th century. This old technology is used in making artistic woods, weapons, musical instruments, and water vessels.

- Smoothen the wood through planing, apply the right pressure and a softening agent, and expose it to atmospheric pressure. After which, the wood is dried to remove excess moisture.

- Assembly: The wooden parts can be furnished before it is assembled or after. Irregular shaped furniture is usually assembled then furnished.

The assembly process includes joining through adhesives (natural or artificial) like gum. Other joining process involves nailing, screwing and application of veneers. Veneers are usually adjusted to size after purchase. It is sawed to the correct pattern that enables it to align with the purchased chipboard to fit the furniture. After this, the furniture is examined for a smooth surface for furnishing. Before the wood assembly, dry it first. Then assemble the projects in parts: wide panels or complex furniture. Don't ever try assembling a project without glue. It is the worst nightmare ever. Also, be careful to use the right glue during your assembly.

- Pre-furnishing: After the initial sanding, a smooth surface is achieved by spraying, sponging, and putting the wood in water to cause the wood fibers to swell to its surface. Don't overdo this process, simply put the wood in water, then a solution of glue is applied. The sanding process is resumed for an even smoother surface.

Some woods contain rosin, which sometimes interferes with the result of the smoothing process. This can be controlled by derosinating. Derosinating is the application of a mixture of acetone and ammonia. The wood is placed into this mixture. Once the wood has been successfully derosinated, the bleaching process can begin. There are three major ways to bleach a wood. One is spraying the desired color on the wood, next is sponging the mixed chemical on the wood. Lastly, you could dip the wood into a mixture of bleaching agent and water such as hydrogen peroxide.

- Surface finishing: The final finishing process involves coating. Coating is a more lasting form of wood coloration. After the product is assembled, the coating is applied. The coating could include fillers, glazes, sealers, paints, vanishes and other finishes.

Coating can be of any pigment, either solvent or water-based. It is usually applied with a spray, painting brush, or roller machine.

The coating can also be done before the wood is assembled but in such a case, the wood is to be placed on a flat line table for spraying.

- Joinery: In woodworking, this involves joining different parts of wood to produce more complex items. For example, the joining of different wood types to make a frame or a bed. Some wood joints can employ fasteners, and adhesives. Before the use of adhesives, joining was mostly done with nails and hammers. The woods to be joined are placed over each other and the nail is placed over the wood and hammered at the spot of joining. This form of joinery is still used today, alongside other forms like wooden joints. The wooden joints are characterized by strength, flexibility, toughness and appearance. All these methods and types of joinery depend on the project at hand. The joinery through adhesives like glue is unacceptable or unworkable in a place where the humidity level is harsh and the glue could lose its stickiness.
- Cutting: Cutting is a very close synonym of sawing in woodworking. However, it involves the intricacies of making specific divides through the wood. This is the first challenge every woodworker will have to deal with in the journey of woodworking. Making clean straight, clear

cuts could be very challenging and a huge problem. One first issue in cutting is getting the actual size of wood for a project.

- Drying: Wood is just like a moisture sponge; it slowly absorbs and loses moisture. If you have a wet wood, you will need this knowledge. Woods are dried using a drying kiln or oven that is fired by a boiler. The fuel is the only wood waste. You could also expose the wood to sunlight, though it will take a longer time to have the effect a drying kiln will have on the wood. Understanding the wily ways of wet wood can keep you ahead from making a lot of mistakes. The best method to save all manner of stories is to apply heat, air and allow time. All three elements work together to help you achieve a dry wood.

- Drilling: Here is another technique you can get in trouble with. Okay, not to scare you, but drilling could be so tricky. Drilling involves making holes in a wood for inserting bits or putting screws. It could also be done to make the design of art. There are different types of holes that are drilled for different occasions.

You need to position your body properly when set to drill; you should be holding the drill at 90 degrees from the work surface. Don't forget your safety tools when drilling.

- Gluing: This is a process involved in the assembling of woods. It is the act of fastening wood by applying glue. This process isn't only used in assembling woods but is also used in designs. Gluing is very important when doing art with wood. It allows you to be flexible and quicker. Before gluing, wet the surface of the wood with a damp cloth. After applying the glue, clamp the pieces together immediately and allow them to dry for some time. Be careful when gluing, as glue stains could be very difficult to get rid off and could make a mess of your work.

- Ripping: This is a type of cut that divides a piece of wood parallel to the grain. The ripping saw always lifts off small splinters of wood. Ripping hardwood can be a big task; make sure to use a 24-tooth to 30-tooth blade. For plywood, use 40-80 tooth blade. Each saw rips a wood in different ways.

- Pilot hole: It is a small hole drilled into a bit of construction; it is to guide the drill and prepare the wood for a larger drill. The aim is to make the larger drilling easier, just like digging the ground a lot so you can dig at that spot for a borehole. It is also a small hole made to fit in a screw to prevent breaking a screw. When a screw is driven into the wood without a pilot hole, it can cause a wedge as you can't apply the right pressure with your hands, but the drill helps you apply sufficient pressure to create a screw hole in the wood.

Chapter 3

Woodworking Tips and Tricks

Woodworking can be quite challenging and involves a number a processes that could be time taking. If you have a large number of goods to meet, you'll definitely need a shorter trick to meet up with your tasks and deliver early. You'll need tricks and tips that will save you time and make work easier for you.

There are more than one ways to do something, you only need to discover it. This is what woodworking is about. You can get to discover by research or practice. Lots of supposed professional finishes and projects are really doable if you know the easy secrets of the trade.

The tips listed here are tips practiced by professionals. They are very simple and highly relatable.

1. Wood layout—triangle registration: When laying out wood, it is easy to get the pieces mixed up, especially when there are multiple cuts of similar length. An easier way to build is by using triangular shape. Although some persons use

numbering, it could be quite stressful trying to align the numbers and what they imply. It gets more difficult if you have left it off for a long time or they are so many wood pieces. When you use the triangle registration method, you can quickly visualize the position of all the pieces of wood, in a way, you get to assemble the whole piece of wood in your head. This way, you get to easily gather all of them at once and quickly reassemble your work.

To achieve this, use a straight edge to scribe a triangle on your wood as it is lying on the correct position, that is the position you will be joining with another or doing the carvings. Mark it at the position of joining and there you have it.

Triangle registration makes it easier for even the most complex glue-ups to be properly referenced. No matter the project you are working on, the triangle registration mark is a great tool to use for boards, woods, name it.

2. Marking cut lines: When measuring your wooden material to cut, it is very helpful to tick marks on the sides you want to cut on. This should be done after measuring; it saves you time to keep

remeasuring. Sometimes, it is possible to forget the measurement you intended to use to measure your material. This confusion can keep you really stressed. You spend time trying to fix the problem instead of moving on to the next step; this can prove to be really tiring. However, you can avert this stress by marking the material at the point you intend to cut the wood. You could also use this mark to identify the thickness of the blade you are cutting with. The divergence between the left and right sides of the saw teeth and any cutting will result in some loss of wood that is turned eventually to saw dust. Marking at exactly the point you want to cut can lead to inaccuracy during your cutting. It is always advisable to measure the piece and make two ticks. One on the side of the measured line, which indicates which side to cut on, the next should be made on only a small tick using the blade knife. Mark the wood not too far from the former one.

3. Straight lines on dowels: This is another mark registration but one that is mostly made on a dowel. Making a straight line on a dowel can be

quite stressful and challenging as it tends to turn in every short while. It can prove to be a very tough task, even with all the great tools you have at your disposal; however, it helps you organize your working process. This is achieved by placing the dowel on a straight slotted surface. In your workshop, you could use a table saw and lay your pencil against the dowel to create a line. This trick works well on all types of cylindrical objects; you need to put a bisecting line.

4. Glue cleanup: Glue is one of the most commonly used tools in woodworking. As an adhesive, glue can get really messy during application. It is very easy to clean off a glue spillage once the glue is still wet. It is just as easy as cleaning spilled water with a napkin or getting rid of sawdust. It is easily cleaned by using sawdust to absorb the excessive glue. Avoid using a wet napkin or any wet substance to clean the wood, as it can cause the wood to swell and make a mess of your finishings. Getting it off your hands is even much easier. You can easily remove it by rubbing your hands together. However, when it becomes dry,

you can peel it off your hands. Immediately it becomes dry, the glue becomes stiff and flakes off. You could also use a heat gun to warm the part where there are adhesive stains and try removing it.

5. Keep slippery glue-ups steady: Sometimes, your glue job might fail to go as smoothly as it ought and tend to slip apart when clamped together. This slippery occurrence can be very painful and sometimes it could happen very repeatedly that it gets frustrating. In such a situation, hold your peace and allow the glue to dry and flake off. Next, sprinkle salt to the glue and resume clamping. The salt acts like a hinge that prevents the wood from sliding around. This slippery incidence tends to occur when you are trying to clamp so many pieces simultaneously. After clamping, the salt enters into the wood and is invincible from the outside.

6. Story stick: Asides from marking cutting lines, this is another way to cut down the continuous measurement of your material and help you

cover for forgetful moments. You can make a story stick. This is a measured reference that can be easily made out of any scraped scrap lying around.

Story sticks are more specific when it comes to cutting lines; they mark it just as you want it to be. It is only less cumbersome than a tape measure. Once you mark the measurement, there is no chance to misread it.

Story sticks are also a great idea for drilling holes or openings at your measured mark. It is a trusted drill guide.

7. Wax paper cover: There are a number of mistakes that are quite common in woodworking, one of which includes accidentally gluing your work on your bench. This mistake doesn't happen every time but can be highly consequential. It happens when you leave your wood to dry on the bench after gluing; it could also happen through glue drops on the bench. One way to avert such happening is keeping a roll of wax under your glue-up. It will not only keep your workbench clean but help you to catch glue drips. It will also

prevent your work from sticking to the bench when you are drying. You can unroll the wax paper and trim it to the specific space you are trimming.

8. Hold glue-ups instantly: Glue-ups could take a lot of time, depending on the type of wood and glue you are using. If you have many projects, this could delay you from moving quickly to the next build without crushing the whole clamp. You surely need a great alternative to this. Hot glue is a great crutch to use with wood glue; it holds up the glue-up instantly.

To achieve this, plug your hot glue iron into electricity and allow it to get hot before you start to apply the wood glue. Ensure to leave small gaps in the place to be glued. Add a squirt of hot glue in the gaps of the wood glue. After that, immediately clamp your wood pieces together with great strength and hold it in place till it becomes stronger. However, it is very important that you exercise some level of patience. Rushing could give you stitches. The best clamping takes time to achieve but could be faster.

9. Drill depth: There are different depths of holes. Some are very deep and runs through to the end of the material. While on the other hand, not all holes will be drilled through. Some are very shallow, while others run deeper. Hence, you have to determine how deep you want your hole to be before drilling. There are a few materials that can be used in drilling holes in wood pieces. One such material is the drill press. Using the press is very much easy; it is also easier to make stops on a drill press and get the perfect hole depth you want. However, a drill press cannot be used for all projects and all wooden pieces. This depends heavily on the size of the material and type of project. Before the drilling process begins, it is very important to create a depth mark using a depth marker for a handheld drill.

10. Sandpaper organization: Having many grits of sandpaper can be a really good thing as it allows you to make different and unique grits on your wood. However, it becomes terrible when you want to use them and realize that they are all mixed up. It is very important that you place and

arrange all the sandpapers according to their grits. Having an organized place to keep your sandpapers helps you get them in reach easily.

11. Getting rid of pencil marks: To get pencil marks off your wood can be quite challenging. Hence it would help if you used masking tapes when making marks for drills and cuts. However, if the marks are already on the wood, you can use denatured alcohol on a rag. Also, make sure to pick the marking object carefully. Do not make a mark that will be hard to clean. Sanding with plain sandpaper should also help.

12. Refinishing wood with coconut oil: It helps give your finish a perfect shine. It is used to create one of the best, most versatile finishes. It is much more resultful than the traditional oil. It hides imperfections so well. Just spray this on the surface of your finish. Also, you could use this knowledge on the old pieces of furniture you have at home. To achieve this, sand the surface of the furniture and clean it with warm soapy water. You can go on to add the coconut oil. The purpose of this oil is to revamp the wood and

rehydrate it. Take a clean dry rag and put it into your jar of coconut oil. After that, buff it. It also helps take away the smell of old musty furniture. To give your furniture a super facelift, you can apply a thin coat of wax and watch your furniture glow.

13. Graphics on wood: Select your favorite graphic picture. If your chosen graphic design has words in it, make sure you print it backward, that is, in reverse. Some websites offer this download option to make it easier for people to access graphics and use them on wood. Cut out a piece of freezer paper, make it the size of a standard paper then place it in an inkjet printer so that the image prints on the waxy side. The inkjet printer is very much ideal. Don't try this with a laser printer. Now that you have gotten the image printed, place it on the furniture when it is still wet and press it in with a very hard object until the image laps and is well replicated on the furniture. Don't lift it and continue pressing; you might replicate it on more than one place on the furniture. Apply any wood sealer of your choice.

For me, it is a Minwax satin finish. After this, make sure to sand it lightly.

14. Color washing the darn door: Color washing is an alternative for painting or staining, a perfect one at that. This is for you if you are a lover of not so conventional results. To begin, mix your paint in a pail and take a wet washcloth. Dip it into the bucket of paint. You need a very small quantity of paint to use the cover of the bucket, a paint tray to pour out a small quantity of paint. Just the perfect size you need. This is so we won't dip the whole of the rag into the paint. Now take a paintbrush and begin to apply small amounts of paint to the board in small sections. You are not coating the whole piece, just a little layer. Then apply the rag on the board and wipe the paint in the grain's direction to achieve a uniform finish. Continue working and keeping applying the paint in low quantity to take the color off easily. Painting a door could give you a sharp and bright color.

15. Avoid runs and sags: One problem that seems mostly unavoidable to woodworkers during

finishing is having runs and sags. These runs can be very noticeable and unattractive. You should never have runs or sags in your finish, whether you are spraying or brushing. It is easier to avert if you are painting in reflected light. Hence, you will be able to see every impending run and sag, so you brush it evenly. You might need to position yourself to easily see the brushing or painting to remove the excesses. If the runs or sags eventually happen, allow it to dry well. You could leave it for a couple of days. Then scrape or sand it away, after which you carefully add a fresh coat to the finish to make it look good. This extra stress could be very stressful and painful when you realize you could have possibly avoided it. So, you shouldn't let them happen in the first place.

16. Sanding made easier: Sanding can be quite demanding and stressful; for faster results, use a sanding block. It distributes the pressure evenly and helps you maintain a flatter surface than the sandpaper would. Sand with the grain to remove all cross-grain scratches. To sand painted

surfaces, buy clog-resistant sandpaper. It will help build up the paint faster and more effectively than the sandpaper will.

17. Avoid drywall screws for woodworking: Use the traditional woodscrew when screwing two different kinds of wood together. Avoid using the drywall screws as it is threaded full length. The top threads tend to grip the first board it enters and can force two pieces of wood apart slightly because you have threads in both boards. However, the wood crew has a smooth shank and won't grip the first board like the drywall screw. It is easier to clamp two pieces of wood together with this type of screw.

You should also avoid drywall screws because they possess hardened, brittle shafts that can break during installation, especially when screwed into hardwoods. Removing them from a finished material is nearly impossible and could damage the furniture's surface.

Woodscrews are much stronger and break-resistant because they are made of thicker metal. The only disadvantage of using the woodscrew is that it requires a pilot hole for the threads. However, a drywall screw doesn't require all of these tasks. You can't trade quality for ease.

18. Know your wood's moisture content: You need to know the correct moisture content for each piece of wood you are working on to determine the level of pressure required to attain the kind of result you desire. If the wood is too dry, it could easily crack. If the wood is too moist, the wood will shrink or warp. You wouldn't want any of this to happen, so you must know your wood moisture content to be able to evenly influence it to get the result you want. Professionals say a large part of woodwork problems is caused by poor moisture. There is no even moisture all wood should have. It all determines the quality of the project. Know the moisture content of a wood before you pick it up for use. One easy way to avoid a ruined project caused by poor moisture is by using a moisture meter. Even when you are using two different kinds of wood, endeavor to check out their moisture level.

19. Keep an orderly and clean workplace: Keeping your workplace clean starts from clearing clutters. Yes! As simple as that. One common dirt from the workshop is sawdust and saw thread. Park the sawdust immediately after working. A disordered workplace will keep you unproductive. Hence, make sure you have everything in place, from the tools to the instruments. Have a designated place to store your tools.

20. Keep a well-lit shop: Illumination is very important in woodworking. You have to be sure your workplace is very illuminated to avoid casting shadows and resultant errors that could come as a result of poor illumination. You can consider putting overhead lighting, focused lighting and on-tool lights. You can also paint your walls and ceilings with bright colors like white to help diffuse the light.

21. Keep your blades sharp: Edgy blades could also spoil the finishing or cutting process. Dull tools like chisels and scrapers could tear at the wood fibers and cause an unprofessional and fuzzy

look. For clean cuts, endeavor to sharpen your tools. Tools with chipped mouths could be sharpened by bench grinders; avoid letting your tool get too hot when using a bench grinder. Once it gets hot, you could dip it in a bowl of coal-water for a while.

A Short message from the Author:

Hey, I hope you are enjoying the book? I would love to hear your thoughts!

Many readers do not know how hard reviews are to come by and how much they help an author.

I would be incredibly grateful if you could take just 60 seconds to write a short review on Amazon, even if it is a few sentences!

\>> Click here to leave a quick review

Thanks for the time taken to share your thoughts!

Chapter 4

Getting Started with Woodworking

Basic Woodworking Tools and Supplies

You are probably overwhelmed by the large array of tools in the market, and you don't know which is important and which is not. The costs are relatively overwhelming and you are at a loss on what to cut from your budget list. Here is your savior chapter.

Many conventional tools have been made in the replacement of old tools. For instance, the old sanding tool has been replaced with different planes.

Also, the saws have been modified. There are more complicated and easy to use saws that have been introduced.

They are five classes of basic woodworking tools: Cut, finish, assemble, measure and hold; the tools in these groups cover every need. We will be looking at saws for cutting, planes and sandpapers for finishing and joining. Files and vises for holding. Tape rule for measurement.

Here's your list of must-have tools of woodworking.

Wood

This is the very first thing you need to commence your project as this is the raw material you intend to convert into a piece of furniture. It is just like molding; you need to get your clay first to be ready. There are basically three types of wood used in woodworking: plywood, softwood and hardwood. This characteristic is based on their texture and the quality of the wood. The type of project you want to make determines the quality of wood you'll use. Aside from this main division, different wood species have unique properties and colors that make them most suitable for a particular project. Another division of woods is; Natural and Engineered wood. The latter is a recent type of wood introduced by technology. Some woodworkers use these engineered wood for their projects. However, there are not so common. Your choice of wood determines the beauty, strength, quality and durability of whatever project you are working on.

Softwoods are naturally softer than hardwood and it comes from coniferous trees. Coniferous trees are evergreen trees. They mostly come with pleasant aromas and beautiful colors. They are also more common than hardwoods and less expensive. Most farmworkers have a farm of coniferous trees that they sell to woodworkers to reduce deforestation. You could also start a wood farm if you intend to go into woodworking for a long time. It allows you to have access to endless woods and avails you of another source of income. You could become a supplier of wood to the larger community of woodworkers.

Hardwoods are not conventionally used by beginners, as it can be difficult to handle and design. Also, the cost is very discouraging in comparison with the softwoods. It usually comes in various color, texture and grain patterns. Presently, some hardwoods can be very hard to find.

Below is a list of natural woods that are commonly used in woodworking.

1. Pine: This is a type of softwood that is very easy to work with. It is easy to carve and drill. It

usually has a light yellow color that is an excellent idea for interior woodworking projects. Also, it takes stain very well and it is easy to paint if you intend to change the color. However, it still comes out pretty fine if you decide to use it just as it is.

2. Ash: This is a pale brown wood with a straight grain. It is slightly hard; rates 4 on a scale of 1-5. You don't need to worry about stains, and the wood has a straight grain and a great outdoor piece. However, ash woods are going into extinction; you might hardly ever find this wood anywhere.

3. Birch: This wood is very stable and easy to work with. It easily gets blotchy, so you can't always stain this piece. If you want a change of color, you will have to paint the whole piece. Birchwood comes in two varieties; yellow and white. The yellow birch is a pale wood with a reddish-brown heartwood and the white birch has a pale white color. Unlike others, Birch is readily available and less expensive.

4. Cedar: This is a premium softwood known for its warm, red color and outstanding aroma. Also, an excellent wood for interior projects. It is mainly used for making wardrobes, chests and drawers for holding things inside the house. Cedar wood is a very rich wood with very strong resistance to harsh elements like rain and sunshine. This feature makes it a viable option for outdoor furniture too. It has a property that naturally wards off moths. It is one of the most commonly used wood for woodworking projects as it is relatively affordable and easy to use.

5. Fir: Also called Douglas Fir, this wood has a straight, pronounced grain and a reddish-brown color. Although the grains are smooth, it still isn't very impressive and it doesn't flow well with stains. You will definitely have to paint the whole piece when you are done. However, it is relatively strong and hard but falls under the category of softwood. It is used mainly for interior projects and is very inexpensive.

6. Redwood: This wood is also a softwood, although it is harder and has strong moisture resistance, making it a beautiful outdoor furniture option. You are sure to have your piece of furniture intact even after heavy rain. Just as the name implies, it has a deep reddish color, but you can still paint it if you want to change the color.

7. Mahogany: This is an expensive and uncommon hardwood used in making strong furniture. It is sometimes called furniture wood. It has a reddish-brown tint and medium texture. It takes stain very well and the finishing looks very cute with just a coat of oil.

8. Poplar: This is an inexpensive hardwood that is used for building projects. The thickness and hardness of this wood rate 1 on a scale of 1 to 5. It is easier to work with it. It is always painted to hide the poor appearance and proves to be a perfect choice for drawers.

9. Cherry: Cherry is a hardwood that can be very hard to work with. You'll be surprised that as

hard as it is, it is the softest hardwood. This means that other hardwoods are very hard and more difficult to work with. Why use them then? As we said, there are projects that might require you to use hardwood for firmness sake. This wood has a warm reddish color that complements interiors. It works well with stains and it usually comes out very beautiful especially when oiled. Cherry also lasts long and ages very beautifully. It is a common wood used in furniture making.

10. Maple: There are two varieties of maple, the hard and the soft one. The harder wood can be a chore when you want to work with it, difficult to saw through and design. This kind of wood should be worked on with professional hands. As a beginner, you can get frustrated trying to work with hardwood. Maple, either soft or hard, is a great option for any piece of furniture. It has a pure aroma and is very sturdy. It is less expensive than other types of woods and also common.

11. Oak: This hardwood comes in two varieties: red and white. The white oak is more preferred in furniture making and has a more attractive figure than the red oak. The white oak is a great property for outdoor furniture as it is very resistant to moisture. However, the white oak is relatively uncommon and the red oak can easily be gotten from your wood store.

Workbench

This is like the most basic tool for every woodworker. It is very important you have a place to lay your wood in a balanced place as you work and take all the pressure from the other tools. You cannot stand and cut a block of wood; you have to be patient. The wooden workbench is the center of the woodworker's workshop. Workbenches come in many sizes and designs. Each design is for a special purpose. The type of woodwork is majorly a matter of preference. However, there are pretty important features that a good workbench should have. Even beginners can build a simple workbench. The kind of woodworking bench tool you use should be researched for the furniture. When looking out for a workbench, there are a few things you should also consider.

1. Sturdiness: A good workbench should be sturdy enough to hold every tool. Working on a shaky and unbalanced workbench can be frustrating. Sheer mass and weight are the main solutions to have a balanced workbench. A balanced workbench is very important for joinery sake. A good workbench should be about 3-4 inches thick. Sturdiness is not dependent on the size; big, heavy workbenches are not stable and very shaky. Some small size benches are sturdier.

2. Size: Many persons pay little attention to this. However, it is very important to be sure the bench would hold the length and size of the wood you are working on. There are various sizes of benches, but most are large and wide. Many professionals mostly use large and wide workbenches. Besides your work project, you need to consider the room size to contain the bench. Some benches are very large that they can't even go through the conventional doors. However, a bench with 24-inches is too wide and difficult to reach across. 8 feet and 6 feet long benches are just cute

Saw

You cannot take away cutting from woodworking, the same way you cannot do without a saw in your woodworking project. Most interesting woodworking projects start with very rough lengths of wood that you need to cut to suit the project at hand. Whether hard or softwood, wood needs to be cut before it starts taking shape. This cutting is done with saws. They come in different shapes and sizes and are for different cutting tasks. Below is a brief list of the type of saws that are being used in woodworking.

1. Circular saw

Just like the name implies, this saw has a circular and round blade of sharp teeth that easily tears through wood. Most circular saws use electricity. It is ideal for rough carpentry than fine woodworking. It can cut true all types of woods clean, but it depends on the hand controlling it. This saw usually comes in three types; ripping blades, crosscut blades and combination blades. These blades have their individual uses due to the distinction in their teeth design. Ripping blades have well-spaced blade teeth; crosscuts blade teeth are mostly staggered.

2. Table saw

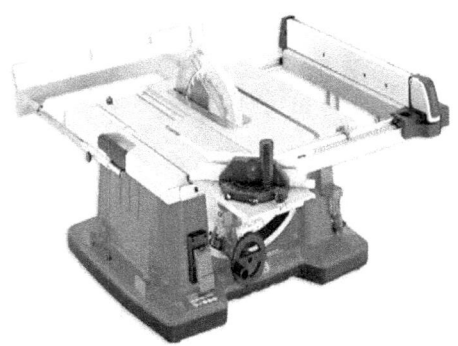

This is a unique saw that produces special cuts that are not easily achieved by other saw types. The blade is usually exposed through a space on the table, below the table. The blade depth and angle is adjustable for precision in cutting. There are three main types of table saws:

The cabinet table saw; this blade usually comes from motors and are enclosed in a lower cabinet with the blade driven by a belt and pulley system. It is also an excellent option for all-purpose work. It is the centerpiece of most beginner's workshop.

The benchtop table saw are lighter and more portable. However, they can be quite noisy, not ideal for you if you love a quiet workplace. Most of them are direct drive.

Contractor table saw are used for quick and easy cutting on jobsites and where time and space is premium. It is economical and a good choice for beginners learning their tasks.

3. Band saw

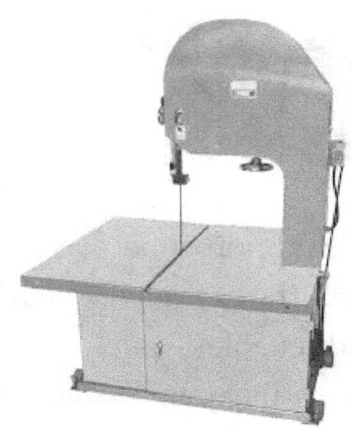

The chief saw used in cutting rough stocks. This saw is a combination of circular and saber saws where teeth are fixed on a continuously looped, flat steel band and usually revolves around the upper and lower pulley. This saw comes in various sizes for different sizes of wood stock and different depth needed. You also need to be certain of the width of the blade. It majorly comes in coarse designs for cuts and fine teeth for slow and smooth cutting. Blade width is very important to consider. Wider blades are great for ripping; thinner blades are for clean cutting.

4. Handsaw

This is the most common type of saw found in every woodworking workshop. It is very simple to use, even by beginners and enables quick and precise cutting effectively. It is also inexpensive and forever ready to go. This is also one of the oldest types of saw. Throughout the years, it has maintained its look, a toothed steel blade and a wooden handle for easy manipulation. There are different types of handsaws for different reasons;

Ripping handsaws: to cut the wood grain

Crosscut handsaws to cut across the wood grain

Other handsaws are dovetail, keyhole, coping, carcase and others. The distinction in these blades is majorly the handles and the shape of the blade.

As a beginner, endeavor to purchase a quality handsaw; it will last you a very long time. Cheap or dull blades can frustrate you by spoiling your cut. You should lookout for a handsaw with an excellent and sharp tooth.

5. Compound miter saw

These saws are very much related to the circular saws. They have the same combination of rip and crosscut blades. The blades are usually fixed in an arm. Miter saws majorly come in 10-12inch diameter. You can use a quality crosscut saw blade. They are exceptionally versatile tools and are replaced with the standard miter box. Miter makes sharp angles 22 ½ , 45 and 90 degrees. However, they can be adjusted for every angle at left or right cuts. You can use powered miter saws to make very accurate cuts. This saw has been advanced and now comes with a flexible powerhead that tilts to each side and sliding arms that cut at extended lengths.

6. Jigsaw

This saw is designed to make intricate cuts that can be curved, straight, or serpentine. Like the lines in a jigsaw puzzle, the jigsaw's blades are very sharp and highly multipurpose. Its blades vary in tooth numbers and composition. However, it is always cut deep and is used to cut plastic, metal and wood. During cutting, it moves in a back and forth, up and down motion. You can operate this with one hand and hold your work with your other hand. It always cut a nice small piece. Most experts also make plunge cuts with their jigsaw.

Hand Plane

A sharp chisel in a wooden or metal body that allows you to flatten, shape or smoothen a board for furniture making. Once wood pieces are cut into shape, you'll need to smoothen the surface and the edges into an attractive appearance. No matter how sharp and clean your blade is, you need to give it that clear, and very smooth face. There are over 100 different hand planes; it comes in different sizes, shapes and materials. Hence, it can be confusing to make a choice. The basics are bench planes, joinery planes, and molding planes, but we will focus on just the bench plane.

1. Bench plane

This tool is used most often, and it is usually placed on the workbench. They are majorly used for smoothing, flattening and dimensioning. There are many of them. These planes come in different styles and shapes. Their uniqueness also determines the price of the tools, but the four basic bench planes are: block planes, smoothing planes, jointer planes, and jack planes.

    a. Jack plane: This plane is used to perform specialized functions like the removal of rough stock, smoothing the boards and jointing board edges. Although there is a smoothing plane and a jointer plane, the jackplane gives you a good start. A small sharp low-angle jackplane is ideal for beginners and professionals who are not into hand plane. It is used for the initial rough flattening of a board. It is sharpened with an extreme arc and has a wide-open mouth. This allows for faster rough removal of wood. This process is also called scrubbing and the jack plane excellently gets the twist out of the board and scrubs it until flat. Although there are scrub planes made solely for scrubbing, the jack planes fit the role. A jack plane usually has a tight mouth that enables it to the shaft of the wood. Avoid buying a plane with an obvious problem like cracks in the metal/wooden parts, missing parts, and broken knots. Fixing the replacement part is more expensive than buying the plane itself.

b. Jointer plane: The very next plane to use on the wood is the jointer plane. This plane is very long and is used for precision flattening of a board. It flattens it until the surface appears nearly finished. It could also be used as a joinery plane to glue up boards for a tabletop flattening to get a 90-degree edge

c. Smoothing plane: After the wood has been scrubbed and flattened, the last step is to smoothen. The smoothing plane is used to finish the surface of the wood. The mouths of the planes have settings. The highly tuned tight mouth can give a sheared surface to what sanding with a sandpaper can do.

d. Block planes: These planes are quite small and can be used to trim joints, end grain, and put chamfers on board edges. If you can find a low-angle workplane, it will help you cut difficult grain more easily. They are new planes.

A good jack plane can function in all aspects, and you can use it for three jobs: rough scrubbing, flattening, jointing and smoothing. However, it won't work well like having three different planes

Orbital Sander

This is a holding tool for sandpapers, especially if you don't want to hold it in your hand and you have a lot of projects to work on. These sanders hold the sandpaper and circulate in a way that removes the material fast. Nonetheless, it always leaves swirl marks that are hard to remove. Most modern sanders don't have the spinning ability, the sand and delete wood marks. There are different levels of sandpapers; the level determines the effectiveness. Use the right sandpaper for your projects.

Hand Files

This is also a smoothening tool; it smoothens the face of the wood after sawing. However, it doesn't have long durability and is best replaced after every spoil. You can see the blades are made with quality steel. You can also see that the hand files are used to sharpen other tools. There are three major types of hand files: rasp, round files, and mill files.

Vises

Vises are used to hold your wood down while you saw, plane, or cut in many ways. Conventionally, we use two traditional wooden vises; face and tail vises. The face vises are attached to the top and the tail vises to the down; they are very important in the woodworking process. You can get one of these or the two, depending on your personal preference.

Hammer

It is also called nailer. This is one popular tool that is used to assemble the whole piece and give it solidity. Many types of hammer are used in woodworking. The weight of an intermediate hammer is 16 to 20 ounces. Steel handles are very firm and is a good choice for your projects. It has long and pronounced claws. There are different designs; some are smooth; others have serrated faces for gripping nails.

Mallets

This tool looks so much like the hammer, but it is much bigger and has a detachable handle to accommodate different head shapes and sizes. The difference between hammers and mallets is their striking shock. Mallets is a better shock absorber than hammers. They also give less striking marks, which makes it a perfect choice in place of the hammer in many projects. Beginner woodworkers should never use a steel hammer on chisels. It can cause a jab at the wood and lead to a rough finish. It has a better effect with mallet.

Power Drill

There are a lot of electric powered drills used in workshops today for many reasons. Drills are not just for making holes but for making all sorts of attachments into other tools. Corded drills are known to last better and longer. They also work more effectively, giving you the right feel of what you want. Power drills are rated by their model and chuck size.

Screw Gun

Screws are the best fastener for woodworking. They can be easily placed temporarily and disassembled. They also hold tight and firmly. There are hand screwdrivers, but the screw gun is most effective when there are more than one job with multiple screws. The major difference between a screw gun and a power drill is the shape of the chunk. Screw guns have six sides that make slippage non-existent.

Squares

Squares are used to get the right angle for decent projects and help you to determine places of cuts and joining, depending on the project you are working on. Some squares also have to measure mars on the surface, making them a good tool for measuring lengths too. There are different types of squares for different purposes.

Framing squares: large, right-angle tools for bigger work surfaces

Try squares: smaller, right-angle device for verifying squareness

Combination squares: for accurate checking of angles and distances

Speed squares: allows you to check 90 and 45-degree angles.

Miter squares: best for settling angled miter cuts

Bevel squares: allow you to recreate existing angles and transfer patterns.

Tape measures

This is a compulsory woodworking tool. Every woodworker should have it taped to their belts. There are different types of tape measures;

Retractable steel tapes: these are the most common measuring tools. They come in length 12 to 30 feet.

Flexible reel tapes: get them in fabric or steel lengths, over 100 feet.

Folding rules: they are rigid sticks with measuring marks used for high accuracy.

Yardstick and straight edges: useful for quick laying of straight lines.

Wood Putty

This is a substance used to fill imperfections, like nail holes, broken screw, split wood, before finishing. It contains wood dust, combined with an adhesive binder that dries when applied. It sometimes includes different pigment. If you discover you have made a mistake in your wood and created a hole in a place where you shouldn't due to wrong precision, measurement and broken nails or screws, don't call it a scrap yet. This wood saver will help you resuscitate your wood. Directions for use are explained in chapter 6.

Setting Up Your Woodworking Workshop

There is no special name given to a woodworking shop. It is usually called a workshop. The workshop is the woodworker's castle of creation. There are basic steps in setting up your woodworking shop; these steps are quite simple and easy to connect with. You can set up your workshop all by yourself, even as a beginner. Isn't that interesting? Well, this book is about helping you get things done with your hands, and by yourself. This is a self-help guide to enable you set up your workshop with basic steps and simple tools. Below are the steps to help you get started.

1. Determine a suitable location for the workshop. It can be located at any part of the house, garage or backyard. Most people use their basement and garage, as it is quite distant from the house. You should consider the space your chosen location allows you. You need a place that will allow for future expansion, especially if you intend to make a career of woodworking.

2. Asides from space and size, you should also consider the design of your workshop and access

to necessities like lighting, ventilation and power requirements. It would help if you also determined the medium of storage for your tools and old projects. There should be a place for storing stationary machine, lumber, workbench and tools. A good workshop should have good lightning, ventilating, power and great storage areas. You should have enough space to move around the shop even after you are done.

3. Determine the means of dust collection: it is a major consideration to be made in your design. Most power tools produce a lot of dust that are dangerously inhaled. You need to have a pipe for dust collection to eliminate airborne dust.

4. A woodwork workshop must have a lumber storage, workbench, tool storage, stationary machine area, and a finishing area.

Practically;

It will be nice to have two levels of woodworking, the upper and the lower level. You can use the upper level for small projects and finishing works. You can use the lower level for major big projects and storage of wood. It will enable efficiency and the dust collection system will be positioned at the lower level, hence reducing the noise on the upper level. Place stationary tools in the middle or far end and leave sufficient space around them to make them accessible from all around. You can move your tables and sheet boards around it to do your thing and return them back.

If you don't have sufficient space for a woodworking workshop, you can place your basic tools at the corner of the house. You only need to find a space where your workbench table can comfortably sit. Other simple hand tools can find a way around. Your lumber could also sit somewhere cool, probably under the workbench.

Step one: Create a plan for how you want your workshop to be; where you want each item to be. Note that this is not a stereotype plan; you can always adjust your plan as you work and build. No plan turns out exactly how it has been highlighted; it mostly comes in contact with unprecedented occurences that slightly shift the plan.

Step two: Create a space for storage settings. If you have just a little space, you can use a wall rack. If you don't want to use a wall rack, ensure you find an alternative that is an efficient method of storage. You can segregate the tools by their function and keep them in strategic places. This will not only help you maintain an organized workplace, but it will also allow you to easily access the right tool at every stage of your work.

Step three: Ensure your storage options are rust protective. It is essential that you return your tools to their safe and warm place immediately after use. Also, oil them once in a while. Open wall racks and shelves exposes your tools to great humidity and dust. Plastic boxes and chests are great options.

Step four: Assembly. Also, make sure to organize the workshop so that everything is in place and well comfortable for you. Get tools like benches and stools that suits your height and will make you comfortable when using them.

Step five: Comforts. Whatever option you choose, you should make the workshop comfortable, with enough ventilation and lighting.

Woodworking Safety Tips and Maintenance

Just like every other craft, there are several safety hazards the woodworker is exposed to. Hence, the workers have to pay conscious attention to their work process. Woodworking doesn't involve much of a risk but can be, due to the instruments used in operation. There are several safety tips the woodworker has to have by heart to ensure his safety. There have to be vigilance of supervision, safe work habits and proper maintenance of the workplace.

1. Eye protection: The sawdust is very harmful to the eyes. You need to have a cover to prevent it from getting into your eyes and causing you irritations. This eye protection should be worn at all times, during machine operation and after. Don't remove them until you are on your way out of the workshop. Some of these safety gadgets are face shields, safety glasses, and chipper's goggles.

2. Wear ear protection: Sawing and planning can get really noisy and affect your eyes. A headphone should help.

3. Respiratory masks: You can use these if you don't have breathing problems or a nose mask when cutting wood.

4. Report and repair all equipment defects immediately: Noticed a problem with a machine or power tool? Please don't use it until it is fixed. Using a bad power tool could be very dangerous to you and risky to your project. Report all faults immediately and put aside the tool.

5. Use equipment properly: Don't overload or overburden the machinery

6. Don't connect a power tool and leave it unattended to

7. Be conscious of your extended cords when they are in use, don't expose them to danger. Always keep it clean, dry and free from destructible.

8. Keep your long hair and flay clothes in a cover with a net and apron to prevent them from getting caught in the machine. Protect your hair

from getting caught in the tools; wear a hat or bump cap.

9. Watch your fingers, especially when hammering and cutting. Your fingers should hold the work a few meters from the saw or hammer.

10. Use portable band and circular saws only when the guard mechanism is functioning properly.

11. Don't use your hand to remove dust from the blades when you can always use a brush or stick when in operation. Never use your hands against a moving blade.

12. Do not use an imbalanced or dull blade, always sharpen your blade. Before cutting, remove every metal like nails that can destroy the tools' cutting edge. It will give you a cleaner cut.

13. Avoid horseplay and keep your mind on the work. You can't engage in loud talking, pushing and running while working with hand tools; it can cause serious accidents. Keep your mind on

your work. Avoid and restrict distractions like phone calls and noise from neighbors.

14. Do not use gloves when operating the machine; they make gripping tools difficult. Your tools can slip and hit someone. It is only necessary when applying finishes.

15. Before starting an operation, ensure the machine is set for the recommended speed, and the blade type is suitable with the material to be cut.

16. Always clean tools with brushes; don't use anything moist on the tools, except to oil the blades.

17. Wear coveralls: Work clothes should not be baggy or bogus or highly flammable. It could get caught in the machinery. Wear clothing that will make you comfortable and protect your body from wood chips. Wear high-top shoes and avoid wearing jewelry.

18. Carry and store tools properly. Sharp objects should be stored with the tip pointing downwards.

19. Have in mind the steps you need to take to complete a project.

20. Keep your tools in a nearby tool tray when working.

21. Never work when you are tired; it limits your attention span and exposes you to danger. You can always have a nap and return to work.

22. Always clamp your workpiece properly: You can lose control of it and cause it to fly down from the workbench and endanger yourself. You can use your hand for a small piece; bigger stuff needs a stronger restraint.

Chapter 5

Woodworking Projects Ideas

Most woodworking projects are not as daunting as assumed; they are mostly made with simple steps and simple tools. Many of these tools are just basic and require simple instructions.

In this chapter, we will be looking at various projects that include all the techniques in woodworking.s

We'll be looking at 11 woodworking projects. That's a huge number, I know. 11 projects, explained with pictures and broken into short instructional steps. These projects include simple furniture, housewares and creative wooden designs.

You're sure to fall in love with at least one of these projects. Please, when you do, don't hesitate to give it a try. Let's get into it!

Kitchen Board

Who doesn't want to have such a cutie in the kitchen? It's very simple to make, depending on the shape you want. Shapes that'll require more complex curves like a heart would require a table saw.

The table saw will give you the perfect curves in the right places. Using a handsaw could be tricky, especially as a beginner. However, there are other simpler shapes you can cut out, like the banner design. You can try out other straight shapes like triangle, rectangle or square. The idea is just to get a board for cutting your veg.

Before we list the steps involved in this project, you need to know that there are basic tools you need to get.

Supplies

- An untreated plywood. You need the wood to be hygienic for food. You'll be placing food on this wood. You can ask at your local store for a wood with this specification.
- Sandpaper (medium grit)
- Circular saw, or table saw
- Food grade mineral oil also called cutting board oil or butcher board oil.
- Clean clothes and napkins

Directions

Step 1

Draw the design of the shape you want to carve out on the board. As I have mentioned, the table saw should be used for more curving edges. In a case where you are yet to invest in a table saw, you can use your regular circular saw and endeavor to stick to straight-edged shapes. You need a strong saw that can cut through the hardness of the hardwood. However, you can use jigsaw for softer woods.

Step 2

Cut the design using your saw. Use your medium grit sandpaper to sand all the edges until they are very smooth

Step 3

Wipe the board off every wood dust and particles. After which, you use clean clothes to apply the mineral oil to the surface. You can read the application from the body of the container. Apply until the face is thick and it is ready for kitchen duty.

To maintain your cutting board, don't put it in a dishwasher or soak it in soapy water. Hand wash the wood and learn to reapply the chemical occasionally to keep it looking great.

Picture Frame

Pictures are very beautiful and decorative piece that everyone hangs in their homes. Well, not really everyone, but if you're a lover of pictures, you'll be thrilled by this project. With very easy steps, you can create your own picture frame to register those beautiful memories before your eyes, always. It's also a great gift item for your family and friends out there.

One constant tool is scrap wood. If you have any old wood you're not using, preferably hardwood, this project would interest you. You get to put your scrap to good use and beautify your house. You can fix this project in three hours or less, depending on how much art inclined you are. So let's look at the requirements for building this project before we look at the steps.

Materials

- Scrap wood
- Woodstain
- Rag
- Twine
- Paintbrush
- Handsaw

- Sandpaper
- Embellishments
- Hot glue
- Pictures

Directions

Step 1

Cut your scrap wood to your desired size using your handsaw. Make sure that it is rectangular and 5 cm longer than the picture. Then sand the edges with your sandpaper until it's very smooth.

Step 2

Stain the wood with any color of your choice. You could use a color that resonates with the color of your walls. If you want a rustic look, use the color grey. For an even spread, dip your paintbrush into the paint bucket and rub on the wood surface. Allow it to dry for a few minutes, then wipe the excess with a rag.

Step 3

Use the hot glue to stick your picture to the wood. Position the picture at the middle of the frame and apply your gum.

Step 4

Wrap the twine around one end of the frame and tie in the back.

Step 5

Use hot-glue to stick the embellishments to the front of the wood at that same side where you tied the twine. Flowers are great embellishments ideas.

One beautiful thing about the frame is that it can stand without anything holding it from the back. If you don't want the picture to be permanently stuck to the frame, you can skip step three and slot in the picture after the last step. Ensure the twine is holding it firmly in place.

Wooden Arrow

If you don't have any experience with saws, this is a great project for you; it will teach you how to cut at 45-degrees angles. You can make simple arrow pointers to decorate your office, room, or exterior. They could also act as real pointers in a large hall or auditorium. You'll be surprised how easy this project is if you follow this tutorial to the minutest detail.

Supplies

- Tape measure
- Miter saw
- Pencil
- Right angle
- Wood stain
- Mending plates
- Drill
- Craft wood, softwood
- Safety goggles

Directions

Step 1

Use the tape rule to measure the wood and mark it at where you want with your pencil. By now you should have decided the length you want it to be. A 1×4 length is just perfect.

Step 2

You can cut the wood at the middle horizontally and vertically using your miter saw. Cut the wood and assemble them until you have as many arrows of your choice.

Step 3

Use your wood stain of whatever color and a paintbrush to paint the wood.

Step 4

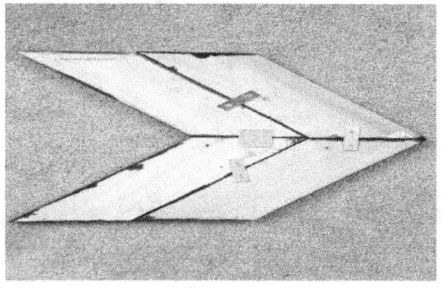

Put your glue to join the woods together. Each arrow contains four separate pieces of wood, so make sure the glue is well applied. You can also use the mending plates at the back of the wood to give it extra strength and keep the wood together. Place it in all joining points until the whole piece is firm.

You can place a saw tooth picture hanger at the middle of the arrow to enable you to hang it on the wall.

Your arrows are ready.

Doormat

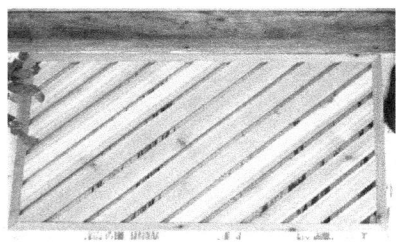

This is an exciting project you might never have thought about or imagined. However, finding the right foot mat that matches your door's color and gives you that look you desire can be a chore. So, making your own doormat is a great project you can consider to solve the problem. The wooden doormat is natural and goes well with everything. It is perfect for a house or store full of boys who do a lot of outdoor work. It enables them to scrape off the mud on their boots before they make it to the house. This mat is very easy to make and requires the simplest tools.

Supplies

- Cedar wood (two 1×4 boards)
- Table saw
- Miter box
- Hammer
- Wood glue
- Sandpaper

Directions

Step 1

Cut the wood in half using your table saw. Measure how long you want the board to be. You can measure it at 18×29.

Step 2

Cut out the frame and glue it together. Use your hammer to ensure firmness.

Step 3

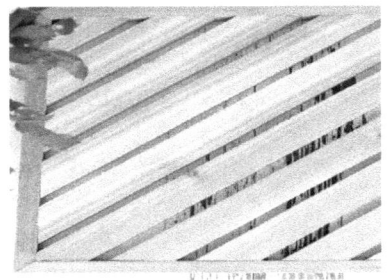

Cut the wood at a 45-degree angle and begin to place them against each other. Use the glue to keep them together. Mark the wood at 45 degrees and keep cutting. Place a short wood at the borders of the two planks of wood in the frame. Repeat this process until the frame is full. Sand the edges and inside the board.

Your doormat is ready!

Bird Nest

If you have a little one you want to teach woodworking, this is a project you can try out together.

Supplies

- 1-3/8 dowel rod, 8 inches long.
- 1- perforated PVC pipe
- 2- #212 eyes hole
- 1- 1×6 cedar cut into half.
- 12 inches wire
- Fir plywood
- Small nails

Directions

Step 1

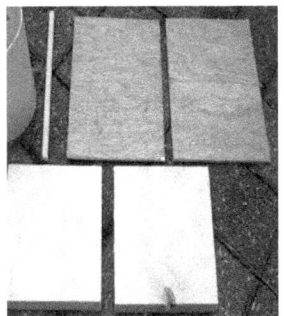

Use your ruler to measure the board and cut it at your desired length using your saw. You should have a PVC of 5" length of 4" PVC, one 8" long 3/8" dowel, 6 X 8" roof piece, one 5 13/16" X 8 roof piece, and two 5 1/2" pine squares.

Step 2

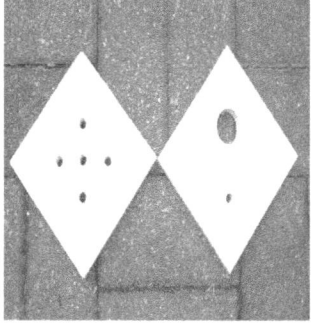

Use your drill to make 3/8 inch holes in a triangular pattern on all the 5 1/2 inch squares. Make a larger hole using 1 1/4-inch spade bit.

Step 3

Sand all the edges.

Step 4

Nail the squares vertically on the two sides of the plywood. If you're working with a child, pre-drill the hole.

Step 5

Nail the other plywood to the top sides of the 5 1/2 inch square.

Step 6

Place the PVC pipe under the roof and use the dowel to hold it in place by passing it through the drilled holes.

Step 7

Screw the eye hook into the roof. Then attach the chain to the hook.

Pet Bed

I know a couple of folks who aren't comfortable with their pet sleeping on their bed with them. I also know others who don't mind. If you do mind and are considering getting your pet a sleeping place, this project is for you. Before you rush off to purchase a pet bed, have you considered making one yourself? It's not complex. Learn how to build this wooden pet bed in these easy steps if you have a lovely pet. You can achieve a good looking bed with very low budget materials. These materials are very basic and wouldn't really cost you.

Supplies

- 3 – 1x4x8 furring strips
- 2 – 1x2x8 furring strips
- 1 – 2x4x10 furring strips

Directions

Step 1

Build the base

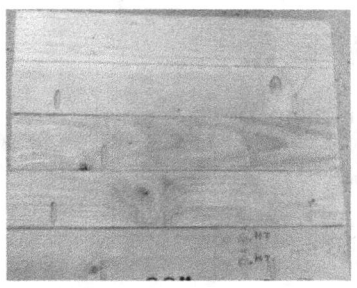

The first step is to cut out the base. Get 5 2×4 pieces and cut each at 22" long. Attach each of them with a Kreg Jig. I used 1 1/2" pocket holes and 2 1/2" pocket hole screws.

Step 2

Build the back

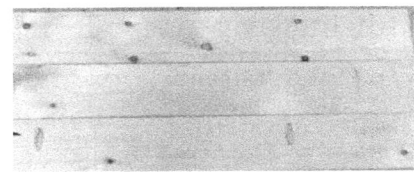

You'll notice the pet bed has a back at the sides. The back of the bed is to be made with 1×4 furring strip. Make cuts at your 1×4 furring strip. Make them 22" long. Use 3/4" pocket holes and 1 1/4" pocket hole screws to attach the boards; you can adjust your pocket holes. Just make sure it fits like mine.

Step 3

Attach the back to the base. Apply your wood glue and use your nailer to attach the back to the base. Any type of nailer should do.

Step 4

Make the sides

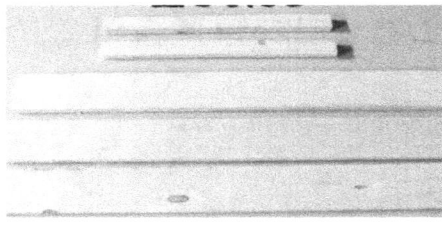

Make each side using three 1×4" furring strip cut to 18.25" and two 1×2" furring strips cut at 10.25". Both sides will also use two 1×2" cuts at 15.25". Try to measure before making these cuts. If you fail to get the most accurate cuts, your project won't turn out as well as it should. Apply your wood glue and hit with your nailer to attach these pieces to the top and bottom.

Step 5

Attach the sides to the base

Now you have both sides well built, attach them to the base and back. Stand the base on its side and apply your wood glue in a line on the end.

Place your sides and nail it into the wood with your nailer to attach the sides. The nails are to hold it in place until the glue dries.

Step 6

Fix the front. To make the front board where your pet's name will be, use wood glue and your nailer to attach your measured wood into the whole fix. Your 1×4 wood should be cut at 24".

Step 7

Make the feet. You won't have your bed lying on a wood directly placed on the floor. Cut your 1×4 wood pieces into 4 and sand the edges.

Apply wood glue on each of them and attach it to the bed by hammering it in with a small nail.

Step 8

Apply a finish

Use whatever oil or paint you have gotten to color your bed. Don't forget to sand the surfaces lightly for an even appearance. Your pet bed is ready!

Bow

If you have a thing for archery and bowhunting, this is a project you can consider. If you also know anyone who's obsessed with hunting, this is a great gift you can give to such a person. Especially now when hunting seems to be medieval.

The bow I'll be describing here is the pyramid bow. This bow is very unique because it contains features of a Pop Mech bow.

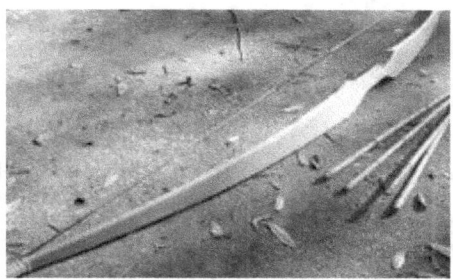

This project is quite technical and includes nine steps in all. These steps are basic; there are slight modifications you can make to this project to suit you.

Directions

Step 1

Find your wood. As a beginner or amateur, the easiest wood to begin with is the oakwood. A fair size to go for is a 1"x3"x8' board. If possible, ensure the board you're selecting has a very straight grain, search for the straightest grain you can find. This is very important; the success of your bow depends heavily on the quality of the wood used. Bad wood equals bad bow. Take your time to make the best of choice.

Step 2

Lay out your bow. Inspect your wood for any splinters, cracks, or knots before you start working around them. Saw an inch off one end and divide the rest of the wood into two. Let one part be 70 inch and the other 25 inch.

We'll be working on the 70 inch portion first. So, locate and mark the center of the wood. Make a line down the plank with a straight edge at two points. Next, mark the middle point of the board and label it well.

The handle is 4 inches long, one inch wide and centered.

The "wedges" are 2 inches long and 2.5 inches wide.

The limbs are 30 inches long and go from the wedges to a width of 3/8ths inches.

Step 3

Cut and thin the limbs. Cut out the limbs. You can use a table saw to make a perfect cut. Thin the board down to 7/16ths inch. To achieve that, use a hand plane. Jack plane is just fine.

Be careful not to cut out the handle area yet.

Step 4

If the plank is too thin, your bow is liable to break at that point. Before we discuss making it thicker, we need to make a smooth transition to the limbs.

Get your 25 inch piece (I hope you've not thrown it away) and cut out 9 inches.

Use your table saw to carefully create fades by moving the piece back and forth across the blade while raising the blade in small increments.

Try to get a paper-thin edge. Glue the handle piece to the bow and let it dry for at least 24 hours, and then cut out the handle.

Step 5

Now your wood is almost bow-shaped. To make it a perfect bow, start easing all the corners to prevent "lifting a splinter" when you start flexing the bow. Cut a couple of thin wedges from scrap and lash them one inch from either end of the limbs.

Now make a long heavy string from some cord and we can start working the bow.

Step 6

Tillering

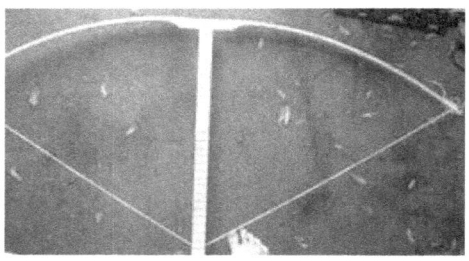

This step determines the success of this project. You'll be bending the bow by tillering. We want a beautiful curve, so get a tillering stick. You can make the stick by measuring out a 3-foot piece of 2x4 and cutting slots at every inch.

Put the bow on the stick, ensure the stock is placed at the middle of the bow and start pulling it back.

If your limbs are too stiff, scrape them to make them thin. Keep pulling and thinning until you have a tiller you're satisfied with.

Work slowly and gently to avoid breaking the wood. If you hear a crack at any time, you'll have to scrap your wood, get another and start afresh. I'm sure you won't want that.

Step 7

Attach the nock wedges

You can apply glue on the nocks 1 1/4 from each end. Tie the twine around it.

Step 8

Sand it with high grit sandpaper to get a smooth flow and coat your bow with wax if you wish. You can decide to leave your handle wrapped with hemp twine if you want it that way. I prefer to take it off.

Quick Box with Box Joints

This small box can be used as a jewelry chest or means of storage for little treasures or a gift to a loved one.

There are a lot of tools people use in making box joints. However, this box joint was made with very basic tools.

Supplies

- Router table and a 1/4" straight bit
- Compound miter saw or table saw

- Planer/Joiner*
- Belt sander*
- Straight file
- Some clamps
- 3-4" wide board
- Scrap board

* = Optional

Directions

Step 1

Prepare the Sides. Use your plane to work on your board and reduce its thickness till you are satisfied with the texture of the board.

Cut out the four sides and label them: front, back, left and right. This will help you during assembly.

Step 2

Prepare the Jig. Take a separate piece of wood, plane it and clamp it to your miter gauge. You can add a plank of wood to the bottom to provide a solid clamping posture.

Now, make a hole in the front of the jig board.

Step 3: Cut the fingers on the first piece

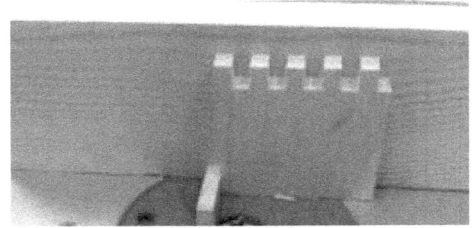

PS: You can use a block of scrap wood to test the alignment of the jig before starting. Align one side of the side piece with the inside edge of the jig finger. Make sure to repeat this process for all woods; don't bother about the excess holes. You can run a square file through the newly cut hole to adjust fit. Don't file away too much, just enough for it to fit tightly.

Step 4

Cut the fingers on the second piece

In this second piece, everything is the same, except that the first finger is a hole. So you have to adjust the offset of the first hole. This is an easy way to do this.

Take the corresponding piece you cut, and place the hole close to the top of the wood on the jig finger. Align the back wood with an edge that will be the top of the box, touching the top of the side piece. Your pencil mark comes in handy here. Continue cutting fingers by aligning the holes on the front piece on the jig finger like you were doing.

Step 5

Test your fit

Try to put your whole piece together. If it doesn't come together, you will have to try again with better measurement on the jig finger and the router bit alignment.

If the fingers are too long, you can sand them until it fits with all sides.

Step 6

Make the other two sides. Cut fingers on all other sides following the same procedure as the first two sides.

Step 7

Bottom and lid. The lid is quite optional. You don't need to do it if you don't want to. Measure the size of the bottom that you need and cut it out on wood.

Returnable Boomerang

If you're wondering if this really works, you don't have to worry. Rather, give this a try and see for yourself. And guess what, it's very easy to make.

Supplies

- Plywood
- Jigsaw or bandsaw
- Sandpaper

Directions

Step 1

Browse out a picture of a boomerang on the internet and download them.

Print them out full size and cut out the plans/template on the page. Tape it to your material.

Step 2

Cut out the shape. Use your jigsaw to carefully cut out the shape.

Step 3

Sand the edges and contours. After sawing out the shape, take your time to sand the edges and contours.

Step 4

Shape the edges. You'll need a lot of sanding and patience to shape the edges well. Make the front edge round just slightly; it will make your boomerang easier to throw.

Step 5

After sanding your edges, test your boomerang by throwing it into the air. If you notice some faults, take your time to sand again.

Painting should come later after you have tested the boomerang and its prefect.

It isn't compulsory.

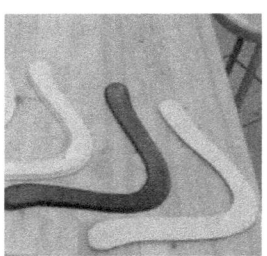

Bandsaw Box

This box with drawers is one of the easiest you can make as a beginner woodworker. It's something you can teach a kid to make. The steps are basically simple.

Supplies

- Light softwood (pine, poplar) approx 1" thick, 6" wide and 30" long.
- Dark contrasting wood (aromatic cedar, black walnut) approx 3/8" thick, 6" wide and 15" long.
- Paper, carbon paper for layout.
- Bandsaw
- Sandpaper of grits from 80 to 220.
- Clamps of different styles.
- Wood glue

Directions

Step 1

Glue up the planks. Measure your plank into your desired length and width, and cut it out. Sand the planks to get the piece of wood flat before gluing together.

Glue up the wood and make it sit and clamp well.

Step 2

Designing and layout. Create a design and demonstrate on carbon paper using a pencil to trace out the design. Trace the design front onto a piece of thin contrasting wood. Glue it onto the block that's been made already. Don't glue on the back at this point.

Step 3

Start cutting. After you've successfully transferred the design to the wood, glue it onto the big block. Before you start cutting, mark all the lines where you'll make cuts and label them.

Cut out the outside lines first.

Cut the lengths next with a smooth line that curves with the sides of the drawers.

Cut across the piece from the drawer tops to the bottom and the side.

Step 4: Glue-up. Blow off the dust and clamp the wood together before putting on glue. Apply the glue in a thin line. Apply a ton of clamps to help the glue hold well. Make sure that all the edges are perfectly in line.

Step 5: Remove the drawers. Place the box face down on a vise and gently tap the drawers out with some softwood and a hammer.

Step 6

Cut the drawers. Cut the drawer and make sure it moves in and out smoothly.

Sand the inside and outside of the drawer with low grit sandpaper.

Cut off a thin slice from the back of the drawer. About 1/4" is good. Save these pieces and label them.

Glue the front and back piece back that you cut off earlier. Be careful so that the edges fit just well.

Step 7

Measure and cut out the width and length of wood that will fit the back.

Glue the back to the box and clamp it until it is dry.

Step 8

Sand and Finish. Sand slowly with low grits sandpaper and move up to higher grits like 320.

Now apply any finish of your choice; Beeswax was used in this project.

After you apply your finish, give the wood a buff using a rag.

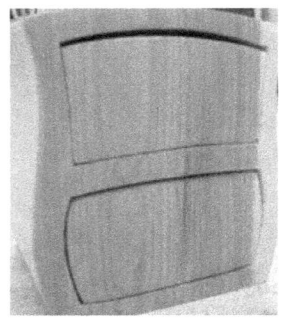

Floating Wine Bottle Holder

This is one very decorative and useful house tool. I think I just love how this setup so excellently demonstrates the principle of center of gravity. This is because this principle rests directly over the slanted foot upon which the bottle is placed. This is not complex in any way; it is actually one of the simplest projects you'll ever try.

Let's review all we need to get to get started.

Supplies

- 15" x 3 1/8" x 3/4" hardwood board (I used oak, about $3.50/ft.)
- Tape measure
- Pencil

- Straight edge
- Chop saw
- Drill
- 1 ½" drill bit
- Medium sandpaper
- Fine sandpaper
- Paint, or stain, or whatever you want to finish your wood.
- Bottle of wine

Directions

Step 1

Measure out 14 1/8 inches. As you take your tape to measure, remember to measure twice and cut once.

Step 2

Use a straight edge to draw a line from one edge to another.

Step 3

Turn over the board and measure down 13 ¾" from one edge.

Step 4

Again draw another straight line

Step 5

Form a 27° angle by drawing a line to connect the line at the front to the back.

Step 6

When cutting this angle, try to be as exact as possible.

Step 7

Join your lines in a way to form an "X," that will be the middle of your 1 ½ inch circle. Make a mark at that point

Step 8

Use any drill you have to drill open a hold at that 1 ½ inch and use a drill bit to cut open the hole

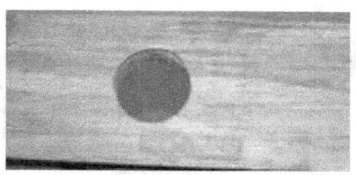

Step 9

Smooth out the center of the hole and all the whole surface of your board with medium-grit sandpaper.

Step 10

You can use any finish of your choice, but I think the walnut stain and finish looks excellent. You can attach a stand or simply glue it to the surface of your cupboard.

Step 11

Now pass the mouth of your wine bottle in through the hole, so that the slanted foot of the board is facing the body of the bottle directly. Adjusting might take a little long, but it will definitely balance.

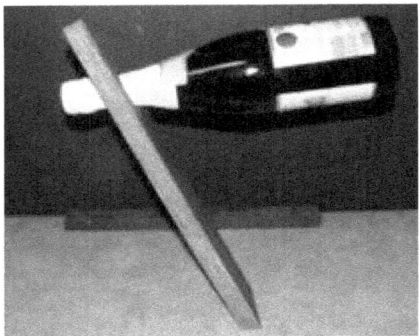

Chapter 6

Fixing Common Woodworking Problems

Mistakes are no respecter of professionalism; even professionals make mistakes and encounter problems in woodworking. These problems could be highly consequential and at other times, are just little defects that could be easily corrected. Having this understanding will help you not have unbalanced expectations and have the right attitude to failure. All the same, the difference between a professional and an amateur is that a professional knows how to correct his mistakes and make them oblivious. You might not be able to totally wipe off the mistake or take it back, but you can prevent it from being noticeable. The good news is; some of these problems can be simply fixed. You can correct a mistake with the right knowledge so that it won't be obvious instead of condemning the whole work. Below is a list of common woodworking problems you are most likely to face and how to fix them.

1. Drilling holes in the wrong place: In woodworking, you can drill holes for different purposes; to make a design, to insert screws, to mount handles and others. By error in measurements, it is possible to drill holes in the wrong place. What do you do in such a scenario? Drill another hole, the former hole will be obvious and the mistake will be too visible.

What to do…

Consider changing the hardware you wanted to place in or on the hole. You can use a bigger hardware than you planned to. In place of a simple handle, you can use a backing plate. This backing plate is not only bigger to cover the mis-drilled holes, but also to decorate it. You can also use a recessed hardwood pull. They usually come in sizes larger than metal handles. In the case of your chosen screw, you can use a bigger screw. In the case of a design, you can use adjust the style you intended to make. You could also double the hardware; double the handle, and double the screws. If the hole is in a very odd place, like the middle of the wood piece, you can cover the hole with a decorative metal medallion or plate

2. Rough surfaces: It is also possible to get the surface of your wood piece rough by abrasion or failed designs, wrong positioning of marks and others. Not every of these defects can be removed with sanding paper; you might have to cover the surface of the wood. To cover rough surfaces, laminate a sheet of wood veneer to both sides of the board. You can veneer just the face if you don't have much supply of wood veneer. If you are working on a chest of drawers, you'll have to veneer all of them. This veneer method can also be used for holes, as discussed above.

3. Metal fasteners: It can be very sad and frustrating when your fasteners like screw and nails spoil during use. When they bend or break, they can become a strong headache. In such a case, they have to be removed and replaced without the wood getting damaged. The best way to handle this is to extract with an extractor. You can purchase a screw extractor from a machinist store

to extract your broken screw. You will have to drill a small hole, as specified by the extractor. It will press into the screw, twist the screw extractor and bring it out. Another tool you can use especially for tenacious screws is a hollow steel screw removal. This tool is made of high-speed steel. One end of this tool has cutting teeth; the other end is plugged into an electric drill and bears a plug around the screw. You can extract the plug with the screw inside. Drill a pilot hole and insert a new screw.

4. Stripped screw: This occurs in two cases. When the wood the woodworker is using happens to be too soft and the screw crumbles. It also happens with old furniture. Before any repair can be made, you have to remove the screw. The stripped thread could make it impossible for the screw to be eliminated. The wood could also be so worn out that it is difficult to insert the screwdriver. You can bond it back with a fast-drying glue also called Crazy glue. A drop is enough. If this doesn't work, then use a screw extractor. However, before you extract the screw

to replace it with a new one, examine the screw hole. It is possible the wood is torn. Putting a new screw in a torn wood won't sit well at all. Fill in the hole with little and tiny wood pieces to give it more stamina to take a screw. A wooden toothpick is a viable option. Coat your fill-in wood (toothpick) with glue, push it inside the hole and trim or cut them, so they are flush with the surface. Allow the glue to stick strong, then drill a pilot hole before driving in a new screw. Lubricate the thread with paraffin wax to prevent the threads from stripping out.

5. Fixing broken nails: Nails breaking in the wood can be annoying; however, it is also very easy to fix. Pull it out with an extractor; an ideal tool for removing broken or bent nails is the cat paw. It is also a miniature pry bar; you can use it to pry up. During this exercise, endeavor to cover your wood with a homemade shield. If you can't pull it out, drive it below the surface by hitting it down. Fill the hole on the surface with wood putty. This is why you have to be careful when hammering; if your project doesn't mind, use glue.

6. Glue stuck: It can be very upsetting to have a glue smear stuck on your woodwork. It can be very frustrating that you can get so confused. It dulls the appearance of your woodwork and destroys the surface. You won't be able to paint your wood with this stain, and it could be difficult to get them out. If you can, scrap it out with a cabinet scraper or dye it out.

7. Dents in wood: One method of eliminating the dent is by steaming. To remove the dent from the wood, place a small cloth inside water and place it on the wood. Apply an iron over the cloth in a circular pattern to make sure it leaves. After receiving steam for some time, the dent will disappear.

8. Split in the wood: Also called a tear-out, this happens when the wood is cut into pieces but carelessly. This can be very difficult to fix. Rather than fixing it, the woodworker should cut wood directly in the cutting board using a backboard to cut it because it reduces the chances of tearing out

in the middle and provides good support to the wood.

9. When a finish is uneven: It is caused by certain oil finishes. To avoid this, the carpenter should start finishing with a pore-filling product from the market. Use a finish that will remain on the surface and not enter into the wood.

10. Wrong measurements: This can lead to many problems, like the drawers not fitting or the door can't size the frames. To avoid this, make the frame and cabinet first and then use the measurement taken from the frames. This will help to match the dimensions.

11. Weak joints: Getting the perfect wood joints to fit is quite a difficult task, majorly a mortise and tenon joint, common in the field of woodworking. You can add glue that helps to fill in the gap in the joints. You could also cut little pieces of wood and fill them in.

12. A table that rocks: Cut the legs to the same length, put them on a panel-cutting jig, run them through the table saw at the same time. Adjust the length of the legs until they are all equal, then use a plane to shorten the leg.

13. Joints that don't fit, too tight or too free: To avoid very tight joints, dry it first, then pound the joint with a mallet, loosen the joint, then add glue. Shave down the tenon if your joint is mortise-and-tenon. Do one serious mallet tapping and clamping to get it moving again if the joints are locked. Always attach the joint fully before you move to the next one.

14. Table tops that are not flat: Use a jointer to adjust properly and flatten the uneven tabletop. Plane and sand it flat, but you will lose thickness. Cut the tabletop apart and start again. Don't be sad or frustrated; It is not as bad as it sounds. It is easier than trying out the first option. Check for flat when you are done and regroup them together. Re-glue them and clamp them together.

15. Joints that are too close: One constant problem with mortise-and-tenon joints is that they always fit loosely. The strength depends on a tight fit between mortise and tenon. You can cut a new tenon or use glue that fills the gap. The second option works most of the time. Regular wood glue won't work; you need an epoxy resin glue-it expands at its cores to fill wood gaps. Another option is to glue a thin piece of wood to the tenon to make it bigger and trim the newly sized tenon to fit the mortise.

16. Lengthening a shortboard: Don't throw off a wood plank because it is too short. Except the wood was for the surface. You can still use it at the side. Cut another wood that makes up for the short length and glue it together with a strong glue. If the board is wider, you can saw it diagonally.

The end… almost!

Hey! We've made it to the final chapter of this book, and I hope you've enjoyed it so far.

If you have not done so yet, I would be incredibly thankful if you could take just a minute to leave a quick review on Amazon

Reviews are not easy to come by, and as an independent author with a little marketing budget, I rely on you, my readers, to leave a short review on Amazon.

Even if it is just a sentence or two!

So if you really enjoyed this book, please...

\>\> Click here to leave a brief review on Amazon.

I truly appreciate your effort to leave your review, as it truly makes a huge difference.

Chapter 7

Woodworking Frequently Asked Questions

1. What is the difference between woodworking and carpentry?

These two concepts are usually used interchangeably when talking about building furniture or making wooden projects. The concept of carpentry was introduced in the first chapter. I'll do a brief exposition on the concept and explain it better. Carpentry is defined as the cutting and joining of timber to make wooden structures and objects. In plain language, it is the making or repairing of things in wood. It involves the cutting, shaping and joining of wooden materials to make bridges and construction projects. On the other hand, woodworking involves all wood-making crafts like cabinet-making, carpentry, and other projects related to making things from wood. In this line, I can say that woodworking is a larger arm of carpentry, and carpentry is a type of woodworking that involves construction from wooden materials.

2. Can women woodwork?

Woodworking is not an energy-draining job; although it could be quite tasking, it doesn't really involve any task or skill that an average woman can't handle. Depending on the project, woodworking doesn't always require a high exertion of energy. In the US, 5% of woodworkers are women.

3. Is woodworking expensive?

Building your furniture by yourself will never be cheaper; it will also be more expensive and tougher. Well, because I have a thing for telling facts as it is, I can't hide this from you. Woodworking yourself could be more expensive than purchasing the furniture from a carpentry. You might be wondering, why then should you bother building your own woodwork? Just starting as a beginner will require that you purchase a lot of tools and supplies, which will cost you a lot. However, after you have gotten your tools, you can set to work on your project with little budget. Here is exactly what I am trying to explain. As a freshman, when you get admitted to the university, you have to purchase many books, pay several registration fees plus your tuition fee. The bill always ranges amongst fat thousands. However, once you clear them and you enter into your sophomore year, you don't have to worry about high bills again. Your bills automatically drop by a huge percentage. Relating this to woodworking, starting out as a first-timer would be very costly as you try to gather the tools and other basics you need. Afterward, it becomes more affordable. All you need to get is wood and paint, which you will still get to reuse.

4. What is the advantage of woodworking over purchasing my own furniture?

Woodworking as a craft enables you to create exactly what you have in mind with all the expectations. You could breathe your imaginations into life by trying to build your own items yourself.

When you go to the store, you would have to get the closest to what you have in your head that is available. With woodworking, you can create something much better and natural. Something much stronger. It has been proven that wooden furniture made through local woodworking lasts longer and is much stronger than those produced through mass production. You can't compare the meticulous effort that is usually made in woodworking to the result of mass production. Also, woodworking allows you to test your creativity and put it to work. It exercises your mind and helps you stay active and productive during boredom strikes.

5. Where do I purchase woods?

Depending on your location, woods can be purchased at the lumbers or a timber shop. If you live close to the woods or forest, good for you. The closer, the better. The local home centers will help you get the wood quicker, as it is in the neighborhood, unlike the lumberyard, which is usually some distance outside town.

When you start a woodworking business, you'll need a reliable supply of wood that you can always count on. If you are not close to any wood farm or you lack close or direct access to the limbers, you should consider starting your own wood farm. It will help you be up and doing with your projects.

6. Does it require a lot of physical strength?

Woodworking, as I mentioned when answering question two, is not a muscle job. You'll definitely need to exert some level of energy, just like with every other craft. However, the skills that are most required are creativity, precision, smartness and patience. You need to know how to arrest every situation before things go bunkers. The energy is majorly required in sawing and that is just 15% of what woodworking is about. With so many modern tools that have been introduced today, woodworking has been made easier than ever. All the same, try to rest well and gather physical strength to work. Also, don't work when you are tired.

7. How long does it take to make a simple furniture?

Making a simple furniture like a chair or table could take hours, depending on the process you use. Furniture making can be very challenging, depending on the type of project you are working on and can take a couple of long hours. Simple projects like chairs take nothing less than 18 hours. Some other complex projects could take weeks and days. A part of the time is spent drawing and drafting, and the rest is used to produce the drafted workpiece.

8. Do you need lots of space to woodwork?

Woodworking cannot be done in just any corner or empty space. A common woodworking shop should be located in a place that has embraced hand tools and a hybrid environment. There should be enough space to contain the tools and allowance to move around and work. If the space you have can allow you do this, then it's fine. If not, consider building a workshop. The minimum recommended area for a workshop is 75 square feet. Ideally, it could also measure 125 square feet.

9. Which is better, hand tools or power tools?
Hand tools have been around for many years now. Before the influence of technology, most products were made with only hand tools, and they turned out very well. Even after the advent of technology, a lot of folks still use hand tools. So, first of all, it is not obsolete, as far as woodworking is concerned. Hand tools require manual labor to use. Power tools work by connection to a power source that allows its operation automatically and any major manual labor. The power is usually a battery, electricity or compressor. Hence, they are quite complex and contain some complicated designs. On the other hand, hand tools are very simple, though it could also be heavy, but its design is simpler. Because of its simple nature, it is always available for use, unlike the power tools that are used only once it has a connection to its power sources. Also, hand tools allow the user to

control the tool's movement to create unique designs and carvings. However, it requires more physical energy and could be very tasking. Power tools are more efficient and effective tools that help you conserve energy; they are also safer than hand tools. But its reliance on power source can be quite limiting. Also, it could be very fragile and costs a lot to fix. It has more mechanical parts that are prone to fail. The decision of what tool to use depends on the project at hand; the level of accuracy and creativity required. As a starter, you can get hand tools to help you master all the techniques in woodworking.

10. Can I build with a block of wet wood?

Yes! You can build with wet wood that is treated. The treatment helps prevent contamination and still helps it retains its moisture. The wet wood is used majorly to create a bent piece. Outside this, building with wet wood is not possible. The wood can split while you are building and make a ruin of your project. However, if you have a wet wood and you wish to build with it, you can dry it using the method we highlighted in this book.

10. Is there anyone that cannot woodwork (disabled) ?

Very much, yes! Although a movement to teach disabled people woodworking started this century; not all disabled persons can learn woodworking. Especially people with seeing or hearing impairment. It can be more challenging for them. However, people with developmental disabilities like cerebral palsy can be taught woodworking and make a career of it.

Conclusion

Having gone through this book, you will agree with me that woodworking is a very interesting task. The processes can be very tasking but fun all the same. You get to exercise some muscles and hone your creativity.

Following the tips listed here will not only help you make incredible woodworking projects but help you avoid unnecessary stress and errors.

The projects listed here do not in any way limit you from exploring other projects. We just wished to create a foundational knowledge for you on the basics of woodworking. There are levels of woodworking projects; there is the amateur projects and the professional projects. We have just looked at doing amateur projects, which are mostly basic. There are other more professional and technical projects.

I, for one, encourage you to go and research other projects you can make. In as much as you can choose a project for fun, try to also select sensitive projects that will teach you complicated woodworking skills if you seek to make a career.

All we have listed here is to help you build a foundation upon which you can thrive and advance your woodworking career. Take the step further by challenging yourself, engaging in physical and online tutorial.

You might also need to read advanced woodworking books to expose your mind the more. Also, don't neglect the place of consistent practice. Stored knowledge does no good, be active and start to try out simple projects.

Stop overthinking it and start now!

Don't procrastinate; remember procrastination is the thief of time.

Cut out all the excuses; they will never end!

You don't have to get it perfectly right at first, so stop worrying about perfection. Get back your confidence and get into the woods. You have to be tried to be approved, so why condemn yourself without trial?

The more you work at the craft, the better you will be.

Sincerely, I believe in you and hope you get sawing soon.

It's all for the love of saw and wood.

www.ingramcontent.com/pod-product-compliance
Lightning Source LLC
Chambersburg PA
CBHW050321120526
44592CB00014B/2006